WHAT ARE TH
DOWN THERE?

To Gill

Even you might read this one...!

Paul Kerry

The Bible Reading Fellowship
15 The Chambers, Vineyard
Abingdon OX14 3FE
brf.org.uk

The Bible Reading Fellowship (BRF) is a Registered Charity (233280)

ISBN 978 0 85746 693 8
First published 2018
10 9 8 7 6 5 4 3 2 1 0
All rights reserved

Text © Paul Kerensa 2018
Illustrations © Dave Walker 2018
This edition © The Bible Reading Fellowship 2018

The author asserts the moral right to be identified as the author of this work

Acknowledgements
Scripture quotations taken from The Holy Bible, New International Version (Anglicised edition) copyright
© 1979, 1984, 2011 by Biblica. Used by permission of Hodder & Stoughton Publishers, a Hachette UK
company. All rights reserved. 'NIV' is a registered trademark of Biblica. UK trademark number 1448790.

Every effort has been made to trace and contact copyright owners for material used in this resource.
We apologise for any inadvertent omissions or errors, and would ask those concerned to contact us
so that full acknowledgement can be made in the future.

A catalogue record for this book is available from the British Library

Printed and bound by CPI Group (UK) Ltd, Croydon CR0 4YY

WHAT ARE THEY DOING DOWN THERE?

A God's-eye view of the world, or what's left of it

Paul Kerensa

Illustrated by Dave Walker

CONTENTS

'Life is a tragedy when seen in close up, but a comedy in long shot.'
CHARLIE CHAPLIN

'In the beginning, God created the heavens and the earth.'
GENESIS 1:1

'See, I will create new heavens and a new earth. The former things will not be remembered, nor will they come to mind.'
ISAIAH 65:17

(I think we're in that middle bit.)

INTRODUCTION

This book could save your life.

… If, for example, you use it to prop open a door in a room with poor air circulation, or jam it into the cogs if you're stuck on a giant conveyor belt.

That being said, this book *will* change your life.

No doubt. Even in the few short moments you've been reading this bit, which has delayed you by a few seconds, you might have been hit by a bus or something.

So, you're welcome. (You may wish to express gratitude by writing the author into your will – that's between you and your conscience.)

Better keep reading then. Who knows what else you might be avoiding out there? Because this planet is crazy. It's blessed with life, oh yes. But from that vantage point way up there, one would have to ponder…

What ARE they doing down there?

WISDOM OF FOOLS

The past is a lit firework: admire it from a distance, never go back to it – and it's best enjoyed with a hot dog.

The difference between a theist and atheist is what fills that gap we can't see.

Faith is like an internet password: uniquely personal, the stronger the better – and perhaps there should be a special character in the middle of it.

To people who say, 'I'm living my best life': no – live your *second*-best life. Give yourself somewhere to go.

Say what you like about freedom of speech.

Organised religion gets a lot wrong, but it's better than disorganised religion.

It takes a village to raise a child. It takes a week to raise an invoice, and that village might consider charging you for the childcare.

'A minute on the lips, a lifetime on the hips': good diet advice but a messy make-up technique.

Pantheists do not just believe in pants.

Laugh and the world laughs with you. Say the word 'LOL' out loud and the world quietly judges you.

Sometimes in life you don't know whether to laugh or to stifle a laugh.

Brains are like chillies: the small ones are the most dangerous.

Fat chance and slim chance mean the same thing. Chances have to be exactly the right size, it seems. We're all after a medium chance.

The NeverEnding *Story* has a runtime of 94 minutes.

They say revenge is a dish best served cold. But they also say revenge is sweet *and* that it's someone's just deserts. Revenge is clearly some kind of pavlova.

People who live in glass houses shouldn't.

They say living on a farm gives you a long life. Not if you're a turkey.

Every World Cup, the pronunciation of 'England' jumps from two syllables to three. Given that this happens every four years, this could be called a leap syllable.

The truth is like a hole in a barbed-wire fence: it's out there, sometimes it hurts, but it'll set you free. Avoid loose-fitting clothing.

Given how popular 2-in-1 laptops, L'Oréal 4-in-1 foundation and 12-in-1 Swiss army knives all are, it's surprising that the Trinity isn't more popular.

St Anselm said that if God is the greatest thing you can think of, and if it's greater to exist than not to exist, God must therefore exist. But Immanuel Kant argued that it might be greater *not* to exist, because, after all, he lived in a Russian seaport.

Pascal's wager was that it's best to believe in God, because we lose nothing if we do but could lose everything if we don't. Pascal's other wager was on Duke Dobbin at the 4:27 from Cheltenham.

Everyone, briefly, held the record for youngest person in the universe. Congratulations!

THE WORLD TODAY

If you ever try to read all of the terms and conditions, the universe will be over before you can click 'Accept'.

The busiest part of any supermarket is the reduced-to-clear section, even if there's nothing there but 500 out-of-date turnips and a yoghurt spillage.

Bank letters saying 'Your payments remain outstanding' are NOT compliments.

You know there's too much TV when there's a Channel 5 and a Channel 4+1 that show different things.

Couch-to-5k apps don't spend long enough on the couch part.

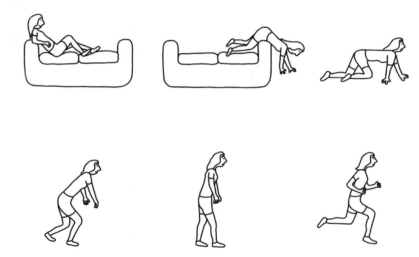

News and weather programmes have 25 minutes of things that have happened, then five minutes of things that are about to happen. No one finds this at all odd.

Petrol pumps offering pay by phone shouldn't also tell you to turn off your mobile – unless they mean you can pay with your landline.

No one's fully sure if you're meant to tip pizza-delivery people. You can tip them a slice of your pizza, but they'll always say no, because they've seen it being made.

Ikea instruction manuals can be very emotive because, well, there are no words.

Not enough people know first aid. Many know second aid – tutting and saying, 'Oh dear.' And too many know third aid – getting their phones out, not to dial 999, but to open the camera app.

Kindles are great, but you can't satisfyingly slam them closed without breaking the screen.

If you've tried fitting a dashcam to your car, but it doesn't stay put or record anything, or it keeps distracting you with a whimpering noise – you may have instead fitted a dachshund.

To open the packaging around a pair of scissors, you need other scissors. If we all lost our old scissors tomorrow, new scissors would just sit forever in shops, like museum exhibits.

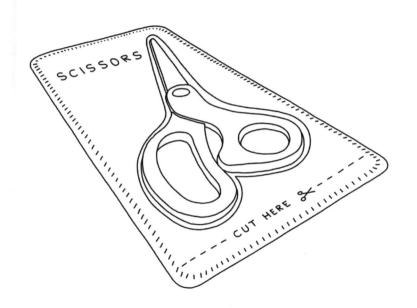

SCISSORS

CUT HERE ✂

Whether the clocks are going forward or back, somehow it's never in your favour.

Many young people end sentences with 'like' and a question mark. Isn't this something we do not like?

The French make 'Voilà!' sound so much better than its English translation: 'Ba-na!'

I'll say this for ventriloquists: 'Dis.'

When toilet doors on trains open like the prize reveal on a gameshow, they need a redesign.

People look down at their phones too much. Look up. Good start. Now, up a bit more...

THE CHURCH

Christianity is like a nearly empty deodorant can: those who think there's nothing in it are often the ones who need it most.

If you're looking for a church, try any building with a cross on top. If you end up in a pharmacy… well, that's just a big plus.

The minister should tell people they are 'all most welcome', not 'almost welcome'.

Some churches have a band. Others have an organist. Rarely is it decided which via a riff-off/rap battle.

Most notices need to be repeated three weeks in a row before they're actually noticed.

If the church wants to take a stand on gender equality, they could start by calling them hyrrs, not hymns.

One problem with pews is that you can't shuffle them forward. One benefit is that no one can turn them around.

Pews versus chairs? It doesn't matter. It's just nice when they're sat in. Even nicer when they're got up from.

Early Sunday mornings, there are two types of people out and about: those on the way home from a big night out, and those on the way to church. Alright, there's a third type too...

45

If any words or pictures pop into your head and you wish to share them, please submit them in writing and allow 28 days for processing.

During Communion, if the minister says, 'Let us offer one another a sign of peace,' this is not the time for dove impressions.

People used to kneel to pray. Then they'd sit or kneel to pray. Soon they'll sit/kneel/recline/text/tweet to pray (delete as inappropriate).

If a preacher uses a PowerPoint slideshow, the wireless clicker will be blamed for everything. This may be a stalling tactic.

The worst word to hear in a sermon? 'Twelfthly.'

Many think a good preacher delivers harsh much-needed lessons to everyone else.

A good sermon is like a diving pool: deep, wide-ranging if you like, just not long.

'There will be a collection to fund new collection bags, because the old ones have holes in them. Unfortunately, for some reason we never raise anything in the collection.'

When we say, 'Forgive us our sins,' a lot of us mean our collective sins – and then hope to leave out our own.

Intercessionary prayers: when neighbouring families, who haven't spoken in decades ever since one grew a slightly bigger hedge, pray for an end to war.

There is a difference between 'We have vacancies for our worship group' and 'The worship group needs all the help it can get'.

Between the sharing of the peace and the Communion bread and wine, a queue may form for the toilets as several communicants insist on washing their hands.

When sharing the peace, allow germophobes to fist-bump. Some churches may prefer to include those complimentary gloves you get at petrol stations.

Some small groups are so small they can't really be called groups. But then some are so large they can't really be called small. There's a happy middle, made all the happier when someone brings biscuits.

If Christians can learn anything from their Muslim cousins, maybe it's the 'call to prayer', rather than the church's more prevalent 'nudge to mumble'.

Church is like a box of chocolates: you never know what you're going to get, though it'll probably include something to chew on, the tiniest bit of alcohol, some coffee and hopefully not too many nuts.

A popular English church sign: 'Ch—ch. What's missing? UR.'

The French equivalent: '–gl—e. What's missing? E is.'

HAPPY SPECIAL OCCASION! CHRISTENINGS, CHRISTMAS AND CREMATIONS

Christening vows should be like wedding vows. 'I, Parent, take you, Child, to have and to hold your hand to pull you back from traffic. For richer but mostly poorer, due to the cost of birthday parties. In sickness, down my back when I'm trying to wind you, and in health, if you stop bringing bugs back from school. Till leaving home do us part, if you ever leave home, due to the state of the property market. In the presence of God, with the help of God, because he knows I'll need it, I make this vow… without ever saying it.'

And if christenings are borrowing from weddings, here's a new superstition – if you catch the baby, you're next to have a child.

Churches differ on infant versus adult baptism. Perhaps it should be decided once and for all with one giant game of water polo.

Weddings are like snowflakes: each one joyous but unique, covering everything in white for a season, fixing a man to the spot in a top hat and awkward buttons… till a shining vision makes him melt.

The ushers wear wedding suits similar to the groom's. That way, if the groom doesn't show up, the bride just squints and grabs the nearest lookalike.

Ballads are great for the first dance at a wedding – apart from U2's 'I Still Haven't Found What I'm Looking For'.

Spare a thought for the miniature bride and groom on the wedding cake. Marzipan on their shoes is just the start of their lovely day being ruined...

61

Christmas: when locals notice the vicar has aged another year.

Everyone wants snow on Christmas Day, but actually that's a waste – everyone already gets that day off.

If you're frustrated at writing Christmas cards, consider the churchwarden filling in the health and safety form ahead of the Christingle service of children, flames, paper, overcrowding and mulled wine.

Christmas starts with 'Christ' – but it ends with 'mess'.

At Christmas, we notice homeless people in the street while we bring trees inside.

Easter services welcome the same locals as Christmas services, but more awkwardly. Those who buy into Christmas (when a child is born) struggle with Easter (when that child grows up, is put to death and comes back later that weekend with something to do with chocolate).

The hollow Easter egg, while a disappointment to children everywhere, is said to represent the empty tomb. So if we seek a solid egg, it's at the price of the resurrection. (The only way to make both sides happy would be if Jesus had risen and left the tomb, but filled it with chocolate buttons.)

At today's harvest festivals, they welcome tinned goods, less so sheaves of wheat unless you also bring a Dyson.

Not all funerals start with fun.

For the best funerals, head to the crème de la crematorium.

Someone somewhere is considering whether to call their open-casket funeral business 'Seeing is Bereaving' or 'Remains to be Seen'.

THERE'S A 'U' AND AN 'I' IN 'COMMUNITY'

The church isn't the building – it's the people who are in it. Or the people who aren't in it, because they're out there, busy being the church.

Beware the jumble sale you've donated to – or at least be ready to buy your old clothes back for 50 pence. (The good news is that they've instantly become retro.)

Car horn broken? Ask the Scouts. Their motto is 'Beep repaired'.

Doctors' surgeries with touch-screen check-ins (a.k.a. choose your own illness) are making more work by making more patients. And they wonder why viruses are spreading…

Never trust a pharmacist who says of your prescription, 'I'll just make it up for you.'

Kickboxing classes involve so many forms, you'll think you've signed up for tickboxing.

Artisan coffee means it's hand-crafted. Partisan coffee means you get opinions about how bad the government is. (The stronger the coffee, the stronger the opinions.)

If your local radio station needs the sound of two coconut halves being banged together, they could try recording a horse.

The easiest way to be cheered by a crowd? Drop a tray in a restaurant.

It's nice when lorries indicate left and right quickly in thanks for letting them out. It's more dangerous when cyclists do the same.

What do they give people at tea dances to make them think the tea is dancing?

Hairdressers love puns, with shops called 'A Cut Above', 'Curl Up and Dye' and 'Crops and Bobbers'. You wouldn't trust a bank with a pun, although 'Account Dracula' might work for a blood bank.

Sandwich shops seem to be able to train bread to become drill sergeants. Or, at least, they can be made to order.

Someone at *Chiropractor and Osteopath* magazine is in charge of back issues.

Religious bathware products: Catholics have Pope on a Rope; Protestants have Archbishoap; Baptists just have the bath.

Houses called 'The Old Vicarage' rarely contain old vicars.

Young people seem to have latched on to Meals on Wheels and renamed it Deliveroo.

Love thy neighbour. Also love words like 'thy'.

'The church is the people' is great in theory, but it makes churches trickier to spot on Google Maps.

THE GENESIS OF IT ALL

The Bible is the bestselling book in the world – and the most shoplifted. Some think it should be taken literally; some think it should be literally taken.

If God is a loving creator, perhaps disco troupe Hot Chocolate got the universe right: perhaps it started with a kiss.

In the beginning, there was nothing – a.k.a. the good old days.

Everything was in its place – i.e. nowhere. The DFS sale had yet to begin. Nothing was second-hand. The charity shops were empty. Call any helpline, you'd be first in the queue.

The universe wasn't just quiet; it was *really* quiet, like a library before it opens.

After nothing, there was a Big Bang. Surprise! Happy birthday, universe. You're zero. So no candles. Except...

Let there be light! Bit more. Down a bit. Alright, let there be a dimmer switch.

The first two elements were lithium and helium: lithium to run the universe's batteries, and helium to make God's voice less boomy.

After the Big Bang, there were atoms, making lots of little bangs. Ridiculous that they kept bumping into each other – it's a big universe.

Dinosaurs aren't mentioned in the Bible. Well, there weren't palaeontologists till the 1800s, so let your ancestors off for not knowing they were standing in a giant footprint.

When dinosaurs went fishing, they had great difficulty describing how big the fish was.

Oh, and the asteroid. That was a bit of a problem too.

Then there were people, and they kept breeding. That peace and quiet was shattered by 110 billion people. It's like a party invite being accidentally shared on Facebook.

Adam's edition of *Who Do You Think You Are?* was very brief. If there was a family tree, he wasn't allowed near it.

Adam met Eve. Awkward.

The forbidden fruit was not necessarily an apple. Some scholars wonder if it was a fig, an apricot or a date. Well, Adam and Eve definitely had a few dates. Really, it doesn't matter what the fruit was. It was forbidden – so no one should know anyway.

Cain killed Abel. Whodunnits were easier then.

Noah saved a lot of animals. Perhaps too many. No one knows why he kept the sharks. They only got away with it because they could swim and kept a low profile deep in the ocean, out of Noah's way. That's how they got their name: 'Shh! Ark.'

Abraham thought he couldn't have kids – then went on to become the father of Christianity, Judaism and Islam. Goes to show, never say never.

Moses was put in the river by his mum, then found by Pharaoh's daughter. She named him Moses, meaning 'to draw out'. If his birth mother had named him, he'd have been called Duncan.

The land of milk and honey was great for everyone, apart from the lactose-intolerant and vegans.

Jokes about Samson really bring the house down.

Ruth fell for Boaz because he was out standing in his field.

Poor Goliath and the sizeist attitudes he endured. He was just big-boned.

King David saw, bathing on a rooftop, the beautiful Bathsheba – an ancient Hebrew name meaning 'she be in a bath'.

When times were tough, God said, 'Don't give up your day, Job.'

The latter Old Testament is mostly prophets and losses.

Song of Songs reads like *Fifty Shades of Grace*.

The woman in Song of Songs is described as having hair like a flock of goats, teeth like a flock of sheep (each has its twin, none are missing), temples like halves of a pomegranate, a waist like a mound of wheat encircled by lilies, breasts like clusters of fruit, an ivory-tower neck, eyes like the pools of Heshbon and a nose like the Tower of Lebanon, while wine gently flows over her lips and teeth. Then the writer asks, 'Who is this coming up from the wilderness?' Well, she sounds easy to spot.

In the Bible, between Malachi and Matthew there isn't much, apart from the intertestamental period. In the Bible dictionary, between Malachi and Matthew there isn't much, apart from mandrakes, a manslayer and a manger...

THE NEW(-ISH) TESTAMENT (RELATIVELY SPEAKING)

An angel told Mary she would have a baby, called Jesus, who will be Son of the Most High, reigning over a kingdom that will never end. This surprised Mary, a) because she was a virgin, b) because it was an angel and c) because of the lofty job prospects.

It's worth remembering that Jesus was Jewish – well, half-Jewish, on his mum's side.

Many think of angels as female, but they seem to be mostly male, e.g. the angel Gabriel, the Angel of the North, the magician Criss Angel and The Angel Islington (it's blue in Monopoly, so that's a best guess).

Emperor Augustus ordered a census, possibly because it was a good Latin word. He may have also ordered an abacus, a discus and a bonus cactus on a hippopotamus.

Mary and Joseph had to return to where their family was from: David's town. Not Davidstown, North Carolina. Nor St David's in west Wales. But Bethlehem (which is not Beth's town – it's David's town).

Jesus was born! The original strong and stable birth.

Jesus' birthday was probably not December 25 (especially if shepherds were watching flocks). It was definitely some time between January 1 and December 31.

Angels visited shepherds in Bethlehem fields and told them of the newborn king. The shepherds were sore (because of sitting on rocks) amazed.

The shepherds asked the angels to repeat the directions. The angels said, 'Ewe herd.'

Wise men visited from the east, and were asked by Herod to inform him about the baby. They did not, because they were wise.

Jesus grew up to be followed by many people. He went to the wilderness for 40 days, to various towns, even to the desert with no food for them – yet still couldn't shake them off.

People say there are no jokes in the Bible. Maybe jokes were different then. Why did the priest cross the road? To get to the other side. Why did the Levite cross the road? To get to the other side. Why did the Samaritan cross the road? Ah well, in the road there was this man…

Biblical names have always been popular, though we're not ready for Herod or Pontius to come back into fashion yet.

Simon Peter denied Jesus three times – although he probably didn't mean it, because he didn't say, 'Simon says'.

Jesus died on the cross. But on the third day... well, no spoilers. Check the Bible. Let's just say there's a happy ending.

When *The Passion of the Christ* was released on DVD, if you opened any case from the shelves, it was empty.

Paul wrote letters to the Romans, the Ephesians, the Corinthians... We don't know if they ever wrote back.

St Peter is known as the Keeper of the Keys – which probably refers to the Pearly Gates... or could refer to his electro-synth playing in the house band.

John had a dream about the end of the world and wrote it down as his Revelation. His dreams about running in jam are sadly lost to us.

HISTORY:
THE LATER YEARS

There was the Stone Age, the Bronze Age, the Iron Age and the Steven Age, during which, in a small town just above London, lots of things were made of Steven.

The construction of Stonehenge is a mystery. So are crop circles. Coincidence? If we've learned one thing from Ikea, it's that you need to lay out your parts before construction.

There were nervous sightings of horned helmets in the fields of England. Sometimes, it was one Viking looking out while another hid behind him. More often, it was cows.

William the Conqueror's motto: 'Remember, there's only one "i" in King Harold.'

Robin Hood was circumcised, hence his nickname.

In 1297, that brave heart William Wallace yelled 'Freedom!' till he was blue in the face.

Leonardo da Vinci came up with the idea of the helicopter. Unfortunately, no one invented the helipad so the idea never landed.

'Say, "Mozzarella!"' exclaimed da Vinci to his model Mona Lisa del Giocondo. She didn't know whether to laugh or cry. 'Perfect!' said da Vinci.

The IV drip was *not* named after Henry IV. (It was Edward IV; everyone knows that.)

Genghis Khan, Immanuel Kant, Theresa May and pigswill.

Columbus was looking for the East Indies but discovered the West Indies – what a massive coincidence.

Henry VIII had six wives, and there's an easy way to remember what happened to them all…

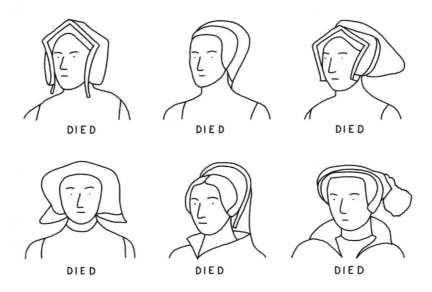

DIED   DIED   DIED

DIED   DIED   DIED

Shakespeare was Bard from most pubs.

After so many amendments to the US Constitution, they should really just rewrite it.

Queen Victoria would repeat her famous catchphrase, 'We are not amused,' whenever asked. Well, she didn't, but her face seemed to say it.

Florence Nightingale, the lady with the lamp, tended to many hundreds of people – whom she'd accidentally hit with her lamp.

The greatest achievement of Sir Edmund Hillary and Sherpa Tenzing was to be the first to climb Everest. Everything was downhill from there.

Steve Jobs' motto c. 2000: 'There's no "i" in "pod", "pad", or "phone", but there should be.'

Sometimes the great inventors are those who come in second. The person who invented the conga was not first in line. The person behind grabbed some hips, kicked their legs out and yelled, 'Join in!'

Most recently, a very clever person read this sentence and everything improved from there.

RELATIONSHIPS, FAMILY LIFE AND OTHER DAILY PITFALLS

It's nice to hold a door for someone. Just not a revolving door.

It's frowned upon to look a prospective partner up and down. Side to side is even worse.

Beware Icelandic accountants. They can be cold, calculating people.

If your significant other wears camouflage clothing, you may soon stop seeing them. Partners like that are very hard to find.

There's a very cheap home pregnancy kit, where you wee on a stick, then wait nine months for the results.

You know you're growing up when you don't look out of the plane window during take-off.

A boy becomes a man when he keeps a ruler-sized piece of wood, in theory to stir paint or prod a fire, but in reality for no use whatsoever.

If you eat a pasty, followed by antipasti, that's a zero-calorie day.

Herbs on fish – there's a thyme and a plaice.

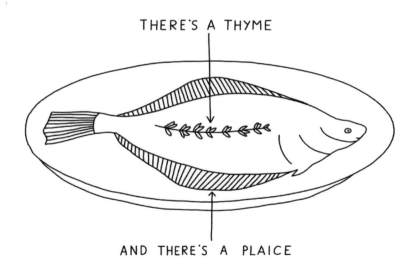

THERE'S A THYME

AND THERE'S A PLAICE

Popcorn: the only food you can enjoy three times – once in the cinema; again when the lights come on at the end of the film and you find it all over your lap; and again when you're getting ready for bed and another four bits fall out from somewhere.

Selfridges sell fridges.

Toast racks are for those who like toast but never horizontal, and who prefer it to get cold a little quicker.

'Butterfly' is a tricky game. Flies move very fast and it does ruin the Lurpak.

Carrot soup takes more energy to eat than it gives you, which pretty much makes it a sport.

If you fill in the word 'CAT' on your sudoku grid, you're doing it wrong.

For some reason, hyphenated surnames are thought to be posh; hyphenated first names are thought to be the opposite.

Sometimes you look at a TV show like *Friends* and think, 'That's like my life, only plural.'

Whenever you feel the urge to Google 'world's biggest spider', do something else. I shouldn't have just given you the idea.

Classical conductors are notoriously unreliable. This is why concert-goers applaud them just for turning up.

No one knows if the Chinese sell Wispas, because by the time you've passed your order down a long line of people, a different chocolate bar has come back.

When you find a return train ticket, think, 'Ah, this takes me back.'

Ageing can mean forgetting what you've come upstairs for – which may explain why so many elderly people prefer bungalows.

Many people want to live long enough to get a telegram from the monarch. So you could exercise, eat better or just write to the monarch.

THE FUTURE, WHERE APPLICABLE

Flying cars are all very well, but they'll need to raise some of those low bridges.

Use automatic doors like you're a Jedi. Just wave your hands, mutter 'These aren't the droids you're looking for', watch them open and see people stare at you in amazement/pity.

Environmental political parties will never get into power, because they just don't print enough leaflets.

If the population keeps expanding at the current rate, we're going to need more garden rakes. I keep lending mine to neighbours on both sides. This cannot continue.

Drones will only be fully welcomed by the public when they can fling a pizza through an open window.

If clothing stores copy the coffee shops, expect T-shirts in primo, venti, massimo and extra-massimo.

Driverless cars will be 100% safe, so long as they're passenger-less too.

Doctor Who's Tardis: the love-child of Old Father Time and Old Mother Hubbard.

Vegan martial arts fans: try tofu fighting.

Give charitably, not just for tax reasons. You can't give to a homeless person and ask for a receipt.

Clean up on copyright by changing your name to Anonymous.

Buses may one day take over the planet. They've got numbers on their side.

'Social media is a complete waste of time,' he tweeted, and waited for the retweet.

FINALLY, SOME PASSIVE-AGGRESSIVE MOTIVATIONAL SLOGANS

Well, I hope you're happy now.

Who in the world do you think you are, and what on earth are you doing for heaven's sake?

Be a high achiever – although then you'll need to think of yet more goals.

There's no 'i' in 'team' – which I guess means don't be in a team.

If you can keep your head while all about you are losing theirs, you'll be the one who gets the blame at the end of it all.

Keep calm or carry on (panicking).

Follow your dreams, so long as they're not leading you towards a cliff.

Think how far you've come, unless you haven't come far, in which case you should really get moving.

There's no such word as 'can't' – except that there clearly is and it's very commonly used.

Teamwork makes the dream work. But then if it's rhyming we're going by, teamwork also makes the bream shirk, the cream lurk and the meme twerk.

Dance like nobody's watching – or if they are watching, it's through their fingers.

Live the dream, even if you dreamed of being covered in treacle and chased down the street by your favourite newsreader. It's a weird dream but live it.

Reach for the stars – but be glad you won't get there as they're incredibly hot.

You know who you are and what you've done – and I hope you're pleased with yourself.

You can do it. End of. (Story.)

Oh, and…

What ARE we doing down here?